# The Story of Joni

Heroes of the Cross – Mini series

*Other titles in this series*

Mother Teresa
Edith Cavell
Florence Nightingale

# The Story of Joni

Kathleen White

Marshalls

Marshalls Paperbacks
Marshall Morgan & Scott
3 Beggarwood Lane, Basingstoke, Hants, RG23 7LP, UK

ISBN 0 551 01184 X

Phototypeset by Input Typesetting Ltd, London
Printed in Great Britain by Richard Clay
(The Chaucer Press) Ltd, Bungay, Suffolk

# Contents

# Introduction

Throughout history God has raised up men and women who have followed His call in a unique way. As a result of their faithfulness, God has been able to use them in remarkable ways and as a result His character and glory have been made known to many people. This series of short biographies is intended for the young person embarking on his or her reading days who wants to learn about the wealth of Christian heritage through the lives of God's people.

# 1: 'Lord, change me'

'Lord, if You're really there, do something in my life that will change me and turn me around . . .' Perhaps rather a strange prayer for a seventeen-year old girl on the threshold of adult life. Yet at the time it was uttered, she meant it passionately, sincerely. It wasn't spoken impulsively on the spur of the moment; it came from the heart. Even she, though, could not possibly have foreseen just how God would answer her plea and how soon the upheaval would strike. If anyone had suggested then that her name would become well-known world-wide within a few short years, she would probably have laughed disbelievingly.

What then was this unusual name which later

on hit the headlines? Joni – just four letters – Eareckson was called after her father Johnny whom she loved and admired deeply. He himself was no conventional, ordinary man, living his days in an ordered routine of business and leisure. Born in the first year of the twentieth century, he was put to work early by his father who owned a coal-mining business. Johnny's first job was to groom and feed the heavy cart-horses which pulled the massive wagons of coal, clattering with their metal-shod hooves on the echoing streets of the busy American town.

He had to find periods for these time-consuming chores early in the morning and late in the evening after school. Far from resenting responsibility when still young, he threw himself with enthusiasm into his duties. Perhaps it was from him that Joni inherited her love of horses. He learnt as a young boy to welcome challenges and respond eagerly to difficult jobs and situations.

And this seemed to set the pattern for the years to come. You name it – painting, sculpture, building and training horses – he had tried and enjoyed them all. When people marvelled that he found time for so many pursuits, he told them simply, 'I learnt my lesson the hard way. It was during the American Depression when almost everyone was out of work. Folk became hard up and extremely sorry for themselves. What were my assets, I asked myself. A strong pair of hands and junk other people had thrown out. So I started wood carving and that helped to see me through the hard times.'

Yet it wasn't only hard work and athletics that filled his life. Johnny's sense of values dictated that he also made room for God and His claims. As with his work, he put every ounce of energy and zest into his work with young people at church. They eagerly looked forward to the treks and outings organised by 'Captain John'.

One of these was Lindy Landwehr and she soon attracted Johnny's attention but ruefully found she had often to share him with lots of other youngsters when they went out together. Nothing came easy in those days with money extremely scarce. No way could the happy couple afford to buy even the smallest house when they were planning their marriage. Undaunted, Johnny took the only possible course of action. Singlehanded, he hauled ship's timbers and huge blocks of stone to build a lovely old house which today is still the Eareckson family home.

They were blessed with four daughters, Linda, Jay, Kathy and Joni herself. With a father like Johnny they soon learned to ride, sometimes travelling as much as a hundred miles on horseback when Joni, the youngest, was only four years old. They were taught all kinds of country knowledge, how to survive camping in remote and lonely areas and how to distinguish different wild animals and their tracks.

For extra good measure, Joni's Mom enjoyed athletics and passed on her love of tennis and also her expertise to her four girls. The whole family joined in swimming and hiking whenever possible.

The close and loving relationship between the parents created a warm and secure atmosphere in which the girls could grow up. When trouble and sadness came to Joni in her later teen years, she could look back with satisfaction to all the outings, celebrations and activities they had enjoyed together as a family, and the happy, carefree days at school in the Baltimore area.

Fortunately for someone who loved the countryside, Joni's school grounds included streams, lovely trees and beautiful scenery (which were frequently drawn and painted by the art students) as well as extensive athletic tracks and games courts.

As captain of the girls' lacrosse team, Joni excelled at her favourite sport.

Attractive, athletic, popular, happy at her

school with her horses and plenty of other pastimes to enjoy in her close family circle, it seemed that nothing was lacking in Joni's life.

But like thousands before her, Joni found that there was a God-shaped gap in her life that only He could fill. No other pleasures, however exciting and inviting, she discovered, could ever give any human being complete satisfaction. An essential ingredient was missing. With these thoughts in her mind, Joni heard of a Young Life retreat. 'Let me go,' she begged her mother, thinking she might find answers to some of her normal teenager's questions and establish her goals ahead. Instead, she was faced with puzzling questions by the leader Carl Nelson. He challenged the youngsters to think seriously about wrong-doing. 'No-one, however hard they try, can possibly live up to God's standards. You need help outside yourselves.'

Wow! That really startled Joni. She'd never thought of herself as a sinner before. Taken to church as an infant, she had always taken God's love for granted. Other interests had almost crowded Him into a small corner of her life. Yet, on her own in the dark after the meeting had finished, she thought about what Carl had said. Being Joni, she had to be honest with herself. Yes, she realised she was a sinner and yes, she needed someone else to forgive her and help her make a fresh start.

Simply, under the stars, she prayed, and thanked God for sending Jesus and asked Him to take over her life completely. 'Thank you for saving me and giving me eternal life,' she whispered.

Joni experienced a tremendous sense of joy that night. The step she had taken was for real . . . and for ever. Although there was so much she didn't understand at first, she knew for sure that her sins had been forgiven by trusting Christ and that He would always be with her. She had no idea then how much she was going to need Him in the years to come.

# 2: The Dive

Early in her Christian life, Joni tried to work out from Bible study, prayer and from other Christians what it meant to follow Christ. In spite of idyllic surroundings, a loving family, Christian friends and boyfriends, deep down Joni often felt dissatisfied with her progress both as a Christian and at school where her grades had suffered. At times she would be angry with herself for being jealous or proud. So there was no room for complacency about her Christian life.

It was at that stage she turned to God, asking Him to turn her life inside out. Probably no-one, however close to Joni, realised that this inner turmoil was taking place. Certainly no-one could have guessed in what revolutionary way and how soon God would answer that prayer.

Soon afterwards, Joni stood poised to dive into the sparkling waters of Chesapeake Bay. A picture of health and activity, her lithe, athletic frame was silhouetted in the glowing rays of the setting sun. Just another lovely summer evening in late July, typical of many she had spent with friends and family at that favourite spot. No-one paid her very much attention as she slid into the cool waters, disappearing under its gleaming surface. After all, at seventeen, Joni was a strong, experienced swimmer and diver and this was just another dive – or was it?

Almost immediately Joni knew something had gone desperately wrong.

The initial brief impact with the water had refreshed and invigorated her. Then she felt her head hit some hard, unseen obstacle, making her flounder without control. An odd sensation pulsed through her body. Instead of coming up to the surface again to breathe in fresh air, Joni found herself lying on the sandy bottom, not suffering any pain but feeling as if her arms were pinned to her chest.

Although immobile except when a strong undercurrent shifted her slightly, she remained conscious. Her brain worked overtime, trying to understand the situation and plan a way of escape from the danger that threatened her. How many more seconds could she stay underwater without air? What had happened? Had anyone noticed that she hadn't surfaced?

Thoughts . . . memories . . . flooded through her mind. Was this going to be the end? 'Joni!' Who was that calling? 'I don't want to die yet,' Joni thought, 'won't anyone come to my rescue?'

Almost at the end of her endurance, Joni heard her name being called again, closer this time. She still couldn't see who was swimming above her, apart from her dark shadow above but she recognised the voice as Kathy's, her sister. 'Oh Kathy!' Someone had heard, someone had dived in to investigate, but would it be too late?

Joni felt her sister struggling to lift her dead weight out of the water. Everything blacked out for a moment and then a gulp of fresh air as her head broke through the water's surface quickly brought her round.

'Thank you, God!' was her heartfelt, spontaneous cry.

For a few seconds Joni's safety was the only thing that mattered, but soon the others treading water round her anxiously noticed something was wrong.

'You O.K. Joni?'

This simple question brought Joni to full

consciousness and made her aware of her own helplessness. Why were her arms hanging motionless? Why couldn't she move any of her limbs?

Realising there wasn't a moment to be lost, Kathy commandeered an inflatable raft from another swimmer, put her sister's limp body on it and quickly dragged it to the shore. Joni tried to get on her feet but nothing happened. A crowd of interested bystanders crowding round disturbed her. She didn't want to lie there, an object of pity and idle curiosity.

Kathy asked them to step aside and sent someone to call an ambulance. 'Hold me,' Joni instructed but was frightened when she couldn't feel her sister's touch on her hands, her legs, her forearm. Then – great! As Kathy hugged her shoulders, Joni could feel something. A positive reaction at last! Perhaps she was merely stunned because her head had struck something when she was diving. Surely the sensation would pass quickly. God wouldn't let any permanent damage affect her.

'Don't worry,' she consoled Kathy as the shrieking siren warned of the ambulance's approach. Quiet, competent attendants lifted her professionally and placed the stretcher in the van, allowing Kathy on board while Butch, Kathy's boyfriend, followed behind in the car.

Joni tried to reassure herself while phrases from the Bible floated through her brain. It was just a temporary upset, she would soon be home again after the doctors examined her . . . but there was no real conviction in her thoughts.

Cold and wanting to go home, she was wheeled from the ambulance straight on to a trolley and then to an emergency ward at the hospital.

The nurse who strapped her on to a table dealt with her competently but refused to answer any questions Joni put to her. Joni gave details of her name, address and telephone number, desperate to get in touch with her parents so they could come and take her home, out of this big impersonal hospital back to her own room full of her own treasures and momentos.

'Hey! don't do that,' wailed Joni as the nurse produced a large pair of scissors and started to cut away her swim suit. What a waste! she thought angrily, having no idea that she wouldn't be needing it for a very long time.

It was a relief at last to see a doctor entering the cubicle. 'Let's have a look at you, Joni,' said pleasant Dr. Sherill and he proceeded to prick her feet, legs and arms with a pointed instrument to gauge her reaction – but there was none. By the time he reached her shoulder, Joni could say triumphantly 'Yes, I can feel that.' It was just as it had been on the beach, the only area in which she had any response. Oh dear! Dr Sherill didn't think that was a good sign for the future.

Another doctor joined him for consultation. Joni heard them discussing her case in low tones but couldn't understand their medical jargon. Even an injection in the vein caused no sensation. A loud buzzing arrested her attention. Whatever was going to happen to her next? Suddenly Joni heard clippers clicking near her head. 'Please don't cut off my hair!' she cried, trying to stop them without any success.

Even as her blonde locks started to fall to the floor, another nurse prepared to shampoo her scalp and shave off the remainder of her hair. What could be the next trial in store, Joni wondered, trying to hold back her tears.

She hadn't to wait long to find out. A high-pitched drill began to bite into her skull. All through this ordeal, Joni had suffered no pain because of the shot in her arm, but she had remained aware of all that was happening to her. Now, mercifully, a welcome drowsiness crept over her. Her panic and fear of never coming round from her anaesthetic started to subside. Suddenly, she had no fight left in her to resist all the frightening treatment to which she was being subjected. Slowly, irresistibly, sleep overcame her, blotting out her terrifying memories of the past few nightmare hours and her depressing fears for the future.

No such respite awaited her family and friends at first. Thankful as they were that Joni had at least survived and not drowned on the sandy floor of the bay before anyone could come to her rescue, they were given little hope for a complete recovery. Nobody, not even the specialists, knew for certain at this stage the full extent of the damage but the outlook appeared bleak. As the days went by, it seemed less and less likely that Joni would ever be her vital, energetic self again. What the doctors discovered after exhaustive tests, they kept to themselves for a while.

Although Joni's father visited as often as possible even while she still lay unconscious, it was her Mom who stayed at the hospital bedside for four days and nights, never going home even to sleep. Her other sisters kept in touch with constant reports and bulletins. Linda, the oldest, was married with three children so not able to come as frequently because of her other responsibilities. Jay, with her little girl Kay, was a frequent caller at Joni's ward as was Kathy, the youngest sister who had snatched her from the sea-bed.

All Joni's friends, particularly Dick, her boyfriend, kept in close touch with Joni's parents while her fellow church members maintained a prayer vigil for her. Yet several days were to elapse before she fully regained consciousness.

Purposely, the medical staff kept Joni sedated with tranquilising drugs so she had only brief spells of lucid thought and then quickly lapsed into a dreamworld again. Joni realised her head was being kept taut in a fixed position by wires attached to her skull but it never worried her for long. Partly the drugs and partly her weak condition kept her from grasping the full truth of her situation. Unpleasant dreams and hallucinations troubled her disturbed brain while crazy pattern formations and lurid colours flashed through her consciousness.

A persistent moaning woke her more fully, making her aware that this time she was lying face downwards in a sort of canvas frame with her head still firmly held by the metal tongs. To her feeble call of 'Nurse', a figure moved over to stand close by but Joni could only glimpse her feet encased in white canvas shoes.

'Where am I? What's happened?' Joni asked in a feeble voice.

'Don't worry.' The nurse spoke in kindly tones. Even in her weakness Joni recognised a new voice – it couldn't belong to the other nurses who had treated her in the emergency bay.

'You've had an operation but we're going to take good care of you.'

A gentle pat on the shoulder did more to reassure Joni than anything else. At least she still had some feeling there. So with this comforting thought she drifted off to sleep again.

# 3: 'Why are you doing this, God?'

As Joni gradually stayed awake for longer periods, she began to get a better impression of her surroundings. Of course, it was difficult because every two hours the nurses flipped over the canvas bed or 'Stryker Frame' to which she was strapped so that she was either lying flat on her back staring up to the ceiling or on her stomach gazing down on the floor.

All the other seven patients in her intensive care unit had suffered serious injuries and were only allowed brief visits from members of the family. From whispered comments she gained an insight into their tragic circumstances. She was particularly drawn to Tom who had been involved in a driving accident. She knew he had broken his neck but no-one gave her details of her own condition. Ostrich-like, she began to bury her head in the sand, hiding herself from the truth.

Joni switched off her thoughts from the effects of her tragic dive. She was afraid to learn how dangerous her injuries were and stopped discussing them with the doctors and nurses. At the back of her mind she was afraid she might die.

Two incidents happened which reinforced this very real fear for Joni. She and Tom had begun to communicate by sending notes to each other that the nurses had written for them. He couldn't even breathe on his own, but needed a machine to help him. From where she lay, Joni often listened to the sound of the respirator which kept Tom breathing artificially. As long as that rattled and creaked all through every twenty-four hours, Tom was secure.

One night, though, it stopped . . . suddenly. Staff rushed in from all directions, giving instructions and sending for new equipment, even trying mouth-to-mouth resuscitation, but all to no avail. 'He's dead', Joni heard one of the medical staff saying.

At first Joni's main frustration had been

because she was powerless to help her friend. When it was too late, her mood changed and she turned in on herself. Would she be the next one to go? What might go wrong with her equipment?

Another incident just a short while afterwards did nothing to restore her confidence. A second man in an oxygen tent and on a Stryker frame passed out and died before he could be revived. Surely, she would be the next one. Joni knew she was paralysed but had no idea what was causing it. Doctors spoke soothingly to her but it didn't fool Joni. She was convinced it was only a matter of time before she died also.

'Why, God? Why are you doing this?' was her anguished cry and it seemed that there would never be any answer.

People changed around her. They either died or were transferred to other wards, but Joni was left there day after day. Family and friends came in to cheer and comfort her but the look of anguish on their faces gave the game away.

'Everything works together for good, Joni. It says so in the Bible, so it must mean your accident, too.' Dick tried to console Joni one evening but it was too much for her to accept. She did, however, try to appear more cheerful. After all, she wasn't as badly off as some of the patients and many of the staff went out of their way to help her, even bending the hospital rules sometimes. Once Dick ran up all the nine floors by the back stairs to avoid the lift, bringing in his coat jacket a cuddly puppy.

'He's gorgeous, Dick,' enthused Joni and the nurses on duty kindly turned a blind eye on the scene. They realised that small joys like this would do far more for Joni than loads of medication.

As she grew slowly stronger, Joni felt she had to be told the truth about her chances of recovery. She couldn't remain ignorant for ever. Even Dr. Sherill hedged. 'At least you've got through the first four weeks. That's a tremendous feat in itself. Now you're strong enough, I'm going to fuse your bones in your spine together again.'

Boy, did that sound good! Joni couldn't wait to be sent down for surgery. I'll soon be using my arms and legs again, she promised herself. Unfortunately, her parents, too, were over-optimistic and when the operation was pronounced a success, they even began to make plans for Joni's future.

Dr. Sherill dashed their hopes. 'Joni hopefully may learn to use her hands again but her spinal injury is permanent.' Joni kept up her spirits while her parents remained by her bedside but gave way to tears when she was left on her own. Nevertheless, she became more buoyant again and promised herself one day she'd walk out of the hospital in which she'd been imprisoned for so long.

'God will help me,' she told a nurse.

Yet, physically she had a good deal of ground to make up. To build up her strength she needed to stock up with good, nourishing food. However hard the hospital staff tried to make her trays attractive, Joni could hardly swallow a particle. Side effects of the drugs in her treatment made her feel sick and gave her nightmares.

Visitors made a welcome change from lying motionless in the Stryker frame. Occasionally, though, some friends reacted badly when they saw her condition for the first time. What do I really look like? she asked herself one day after two school friends appeared particularly distressed.

'Fetch my mirror, please,' she begged her friend Jackie.

Although Jackie tried to put her off, Joni persisted . . . and then wished she hadn't. It was far, far worse than she imagined – rather like a scene from a horror movie. As her hair had been shorn for the first operation, her scalp still remained bald, her teeth discoloured by the many drugs she was compelled to take daily and her lustreless eyes were sunk in her pinched face. Joni's weight had dropped dramatically during her stay in hospital. Really, there was scarcely any feature which related to the appearance of the former Joni, alert, vigorous, aglow with health and energy. Her eyes used to sparkle and her hair shine in the sunlight as she raced across the meadows on her horse Tumbleweed, training for local gymkhanas.

Seeing herself made Joni hit an all-time low in her depression. As Jackie removed the hateful mirror, Joni almost gave up for good.

'Why have you done this for me, Lord?' she cried in anguish. No wonder her friends couldn't bear the sight of her, she couldn't even face her own reflection in a looking-glass.

'Jackie, you've simply got to help me . . . I can't stand it any longer. I'm nearly gone already so you might just as well give me something to finish me off . . . say an overdose of pills. Or you could cut my wrists. Please, please, Jackie. I can't do it for myself.'

Jackie burst into tears. She was torn in two, not knowing what was right. Hers was no superficial friendship with Joni, she really cared about her and hated to see her suffering, day after day, week after week. And yet . . . she couldn't bring herself to do it.

'I'm sorry, Joni, I just can't,' she sobbed.

Joni dropped the subject. She realised she couldn't press the matter at that stage and she herself was powerless. From time to time, though, she fell victim to fresh bouts of depression and appealed to Jackie once more to end it all. When she refused again, all Joni could hope for was that some accident by the hospital staff might finish everything off for her.

This feeling persisted a long time afterwards even when Joni was moved to another hospital. With Dick away at college and being faced with lifelong physical problems, life didn't seem worth hanging on to. Sure, she'd lose Dick, he'd pass out of her life eventually, she couldn't expect him to be tied to a human wreck for ever. Even with the best possible treatment she was making very little progress. It was an extremely black period for Joni and her faith in God was severely tested.

Until Dick went away, however, he remained a staunch friend. Passages he read from the Bible comforted her in moments of deep need. 'When all kinds of trials and temptations crowd into your lives . . . don't resent them as intruders, but welcome them as friends. (James 1: 2-3) You know, Joni, God has let this happen to test your faith, not just to make a complete mess-up of your life.'

This proved a milestone in Joni's emotional recovery, at least for the time being. After they had both prayed for wisdom in that difficult situation, Joni began to think more positively.

That didn't mean every problem promptly melted away. Enormous hospital bills still had to be met; not only Dick but many other friends disappeared for the start of college term and the course of physical therapy to which she was subjected proved gruelling. Joni felt exhausted after even half an hour with her instructor, trying to more her arms only a fraction of an inch.

'Good try, Joni. Don't worry too much', smiled the therapist after a tiring session, 'we'll persevere until you're ready for Greenoaks.'

'Hi? Where's that?' Joni asked excitably.

It's a super rehabilitation centre which specialises in cases like yours. As soon as they have a place for you, we shall pass you on to them. Think, Joni, it's the next step in your recovery programme.'

This promise was a real boost to Joni and motivated her to put all her energies into getting her remaining muscles to work.

Moving day proved another red-letter day.

The bric-a-brac which had accumulated through three and a half months in one hospital ward was stacked into boxes and Joni wheeled to the waiting ambulance.

The lovely fresh air outdoors gave off a heady fragrance to Joni after the stuffiness inside. Lying beside the open window of the ambulance she could move her head sufficiently to appreciate the beautiful autumnal colours of the trees now in the season that Americans call 'the fall'. Joni was almost moved to tears by the whole fantastic experience of viewing the outsideworld again. It raised her spirits and enthused her with optimism for the next stage in her treatment.

Life wasn't too bad, after all!

# 4:  Greenoaks

Unfortunately, as so often happens, the antici-
pation proved better than the real experience.
The building itself turned out to be rather a
disappointment. Joni had been expecting a sort
of stately home situated in its own grounds, but
Greenoaks looked for all the world like a run-of-
the-mill factory or office block. One of Joni's
illusions was destroyed already.

Inside the decorations appeared shabby, most
of the rooms needed a face-lift and a lick of paint.
All the patients were anchored in frames, beds
or wheelchairs instead of hobbling around themselves on the way to recovery. As if that weren't
enough, one of the patients, Anne, met Joni's
arrival with a string of abuse. She was sick of

having Joni held up as an example of a model patient in the previous hospital. Even being greeted by her mother and father didn't compensate for Joni's initial disappointments.

The other three girls in the room made her feel at home, laughing and joking bravely in spite of their disabilities. Anne continued to get under her skin with constantly cutting remarks and polluting the air with tobacco smoke. This would be a make-or-break situation for Joni. She herself had only just survived in spite of tremendous odds and couldn't yet be regarded as on the road to recovery. Only the fact that she was unable to take her own life because of her paralysis had kept her alive. This all helped Joni to understand the bitterness which sparked off Anne's attitude.

Instead of an exhilarating change from the previous hospital, life settled down into rather a boring routine of eating, sleeping and television with the hard-worked staff stretched to the utmost to complete just the ordinary chores. Visits from friends became even more important not only to Joni, but the whole ward. Jay took over the job of shampooing the heads of all five girls. At least a new fuzz of hair was covering Joni's scalp but her bones pushing through her skin were causing distressing bedsores.

At times, discouraged, Joni would argue with

the therapists. 'Whatever's the use of all this exercising? I can't feel a thing.'

'Never mind – we've still got to keep your muscles supple. Otherwise your circulation would cause lots of problems.'

After lying flat for weeks, Joni found it frightening to be strapped to a board and lifted slowly into a near-upright position. 'Hold it, I can't take it any more,' she wailed.

'Don't worry – we'll do it a bit at a time,' she was reassured.

Diana, a high school friend, became a pillar of strength over this period. She was just as excited as Joni when progress was made and always brought with her a verse from the Bible to encourage and comfort her. In addition, Joni's church had decided to stage an all-night prayer vigil for her complete healing.

Although it took place as arranged, there was no outward change in Joni's condition. 'Don't worry,' she told friends and family, 'the Lord's going to do it in His own time,' but inwardly she seethed with frustration.

Writing about it afterwards in her book, Joni was refeshingly honest. She didn't disguise her reactions or try to make out that she bore all her sufferings with saintly composure. Probably that, more than any other fact, has made her writing popular with thousands of handicapped people passing through similar experiences. Joni's postbag remains enormous because she identifies with other folks' ups and downs on the way to recovery.

She might have agreed previously with Dick that 'all things together for good' but there was still times when she found it hard to believe that particular Bible text in her own circumstances.

Her first day at home, as it coincided with Christmas, should have been a red-letter experience, but it brought both joy and sadness. It was great to find herself in her old familiar surroundings once more, yet Joni felt self-consciousy deformed and asked her mother to cover her useless legs with a blanket. A blond wig covered her lack of hair and she was able to wear ordinary clothes again. Yet it wasn't her appearance that troubled Joni nearly so much as the vivid scenes of Christmas in the past that kept flashing through her brain and made her contrast her present immobility during the festivities with the hectic, lively excitement of former times. She struggled valiantly to keep back her tears for the sake of all the family who had worked so hard to give her a loving, memorable reception back home.

No sooner had she recovered from that than

the hospital authorities delivered another ulti-matum. 'No more outside visits for a while, Joni. We've simply got to heal those bed sores by putting you back on the Stryker.'

Deep despondency set in again, and again the longing to end her own life. 'There's no future for me – and I can't cling to Dick for ever. I'll never be capable of leading an independent life. In fact, I'm little better than a vegetable,' she thought to herself. A gruelling operation to pare away some of the sharp angles on her hip and tail bones put her under further pressure. Then, having weathered that storm, and thinking she was at last on the road to recovery, she was back on the Stryker with the healing wounds having burst open as soon as she had started to sit up.

Not only her own problems but other people's chased round and round in her mind. Her sister Jay's divorce had become final and Joni grieved for her and Kay, her small daughter. There was nothing she could do physically to take her mind off what she felt was their hopeless situation. Whatever the therapist suggested she should try, Joni turned down flatly.

Joni's faith feached an all-time low, too. One of the attendants was deliberately cruel and offensive to her when no-one else was looking, blackmailing her to keep quiet. Jim Pollard, another young quadriplegic, used to discuss the meaning of life with Joni. 'Religion's merely shallow. The idea of a personal God is absolutely ridiculous. Get the most you can out of life now – there's certainly no afterlife.'

Joni tried hard to refute his arguments but after she had read some of his agnostic books and tracts, she became more confused herself instead of helping Jim.

Still she felt reluctant to be won over completely to Jim's point of view. 'Give me time Jim. I've still got to sort it all out.'

'There's no God, Joni.'

In desperation Joni prayed. 'I've come to the end of the road. If You don't exist there's no point in carrying on. It's up to You now, Lord, to prove to me You really do exist.'

Being a fair-minded person, Joni still persevered in reading widely. She was determined to explore all the evidence before coming to a final decision. Yet the more she delved into atheistic writings, the more muddled, unsure and unhappy she became. Finally she turned again to the Bible, convinced that God was real although she couldn't understand His dealings with her.

One bright spot at this time was Diana becoming a full-time volunteer worker in the hospital while she waited for guidance from God about her future career. Although she helped many other patients as well by this time, she was frequently on hand to discuss problems with Joni.

'I'm scared, Diana,' confessed Joni one day. 'I don't know what's going to happen in the future.'

'I guess it all boils down to trusting the Lord, Joni. God doesn't always let us know all the answers a long time ahead. Why don't you do something more positive for a change instead of probing the past?'

'Like what?'

'Like trying occupational therapy as a challenge. Your therapist keeps saying you could write and draw with pens in your mouth. Why don't you give it a try?'

Joni still nursed a secret hope that one day the use of her hands would come back to her. Still, it seemed to make sense meanwhile to make an effort, if only to pass the time better. Once started, she began to enjoy it in spite of the hard struggle at first and she felt a real sense of achievement when she finally wrote her first letter home! Another small but significant milestone!

A visit to another hospital for a further back

operation placed Joni again lying on her front for a fortnight. This time she used for reading more uplifting literature like C. S. Lewis's books which began to build up her faith once more.

Because this second operation proved a success, Joni knew for sure that she would be able to sit up in a wheelchair later on. She began to experiment with other forms of therapy, first painting ceramic discs and then sketching with a sharp stylus on wet clay.

Chris Brown, the occupational therapist, was delighted. 'That's fantastic. You've got real skill. Let's work at it together.'

Imperceptibly the healing process was taking place, not of the body but the mind. Joni no longer felt angry and rebellious. She couldn't probe far ahead into the long-term future but for the present time was passing much more quickly and pleasantly. Slowly but surely her faith became strengthened.

Progressing to sketching with charcoal pencils on to sheets of drawing paper, Joni was amazed at her own success. At least she could now express herself in a creative way. The joy she felt in rediscovering her talent spilled over in a little sign she wrote on all her drawings – PTL – for Praise the Lord.

God had stripped her of nearly everything to

bring her closer to Himself, she reasoned. Before as a lively teenager, she was involved in so many distractions, she rarely found time to consider deeply His claims upon her life. Now, with plenty of time and almost total inaction, she could think through the whole of her relationship with Him.

Soon everything began to come together. By degrees, Joni spent longer and longer periods sitting up in her wheel chair. That meant different clothes and Joni enjoyed experimenting with comfortable, fashionable casual wear. Once her hair had grown to a reasonable length again, new hair styles could be tried out. It was a very different Joni who travelled home for the next Christmas.

So different in fact that she resented having to return to Greenoaks afterwards. It seemed such an anticlimax to the enjoyable festivities at home.

'Don't worry, Joni,' promised her father, 'you won't have to. The specialist rehabilitation centre in California we've been talking about has a bed for you. We'll fly out together."

Rancho Los Amigos – here I come! thought Joni. I can't wait for the next step in my recovery.

# 5:  Dashed Hopes

Joni fell in love with the place at first sight, just as she had before been repelled by Greenoaks. At the back of her mind she felt sure she would regain the use of her hands and then perhaps later even be able to marry Dick.

The atmosphere in this hospital was casual and relaxed. Friends were encouraged rather than eyed with suspicion. Joni managed gradually to feed herself with a spoon bent to an angle and fixed to her arm brace. She needed terrific concentration but gradually the whole process became smoother.

An even greater achievement followed. Strapped into a wheelchair so she would not fall out, Joni learnt to control the knobs at the side of her chair and move it inch by inch down the corridor. A measure of freedom at last! Joni could even venture outside the immediate hospital building now she had a reliable means of transport.

Rick, another quadriplegic, challenged her to a race one day. 'Let's race right round the corridors to the front door, Joni.'

'O.K. We're off!'

Unfortunately, the marathon ended in confusion as Joni crashed into a nurse carrying a tray full of bottles and drugs. Although they took away her chair for a while as a punishment, Joni knew she was now capable of leading a much more fulfilling life. Within a short time the doctors told her she could go home. Only one question remained unsolved.

'My hands, Doctor?'

'They'll never be any use. Try and be reconciled to the idea, Joni.'

When the disappointment had sunk in, the news sparked off a letter to Dick, finally giving him his freedom. 'I'll always love you, Dick, but there's no future for us together as man and wife.'

After the peak of happiness at Rancho los Amigos, Joni had entered a new trough of despair. She cared deeply for Dick, so deeply that she couldn't bear him to lead a frustrated life, tied to a wife who was unable to do anything for either him or herself. She could have blackmailed him emotionally to stay tied to her, but it wasn't her way. But it took a long time to adjust to the new situation. And it was a severe blow to accept she would never enjoy the use of her hands.

Joni was driven inside herself again and again to indulge in wild daydreams and fantasies – anything to escape from the harsh world of reality. Outwardly she appeared the same cheerful Joni who was bravely trying to come to terms with her paralysis but inwardly she was raging against God. Other unbearable pressures were building up too, making the burden almost intolerable. Her sister Jay had faced up to the bitterness of divorce and her young niece Kelly was dying of brain cancer.

Slowly Joni withdrew from indulging herself in these harmful day-dreams. The past was irrevocably over; she must live in the present. But where was God in all this unhappiness? What point was He trying to make?

Wisely, Joni realised she needed help outside herself. Diana came to the rescue with a young Christian friend, Steve Estes. Although apprehensive about meeting him, Joni took to him immediately.

'Please come back and tell me more, Steve,' she begged at the end of their first chat together. For a high school student, he showed an amazing maturity and depth of understanding far beyond his years.

'How about a weekly Bible study in your home?' he suggested tentatively.

Joni seized on this avidly. So did other friends and her sister Jay. Soon it became the high spot of the week, challenging and informative. Joni began to look at life from God's point of view instead of being engrossed in her own problems. She saw the value of the Bible as a guide-book for living and realised she had been playing with fire in her early relationships. God had a very good reason for all His commands and prohibitions. He wasn't being a kill/joy in stipulating no sex before marriage. It was an essential rule to ensure their happiness and welfare.

No longer did Joni's spiritual life appear like a graph of peaks and troughs. She began to look outside herself and appreciate how other people, too, had suffered like Job, Paul and Jeremiah, and had triumphed through by God's grace. She found it helpful to commit certain passages from the Bible to memory. These she could recall to comfort her during the bad spells and it saved her having to escape to her fantasy world and dreams.

In time she felt less sensitive and awkward when she ventured out in her wheelchair. Deprived of contact with the outside world for a couple of vital years in her life, Joni revelled in the beauties of nature on country visits with her friends. She became so absorbed in all the wonders around her, she forgot people looking at her in pity.

Another more difficult step was to share her regained, growing faith with others. Joni felt petrified and tongue-tied in her first experience of talking to a group of teenagers. A few awkward phrases and she dried up.

'I'll never be articulate, Steve,' she moaned. 'That's the end of that experiment.'

'It's only to be expected – I reacted in just the same way myself. With a little practice and training you'll make it.'

So the new autumn term saw Joni as a student at college, enrolled for a course in public speaking. Jay and Diana went along too but she soon found others in wheelchairs. Dimly she could grasp a little of what kind of service God planned for her future. She was neither looking back with nostalgia to her action-packed life before that fateful dive nor was she totally engrossed in her present physical limitations, but she could look ahead, hopefully.

At that stage came another blow, not unexpected, but nevertheless hard to take. Joni's niece, Kelly, finally died of a brain tumour. The Eareckson family was under tremendous pressure – Joni's accident, Jay's divorce, Kelly's death at the age of five just after her father had left her mother Linda to cope with two boys and the trauma of Kelly's fatal illness.

Steve encouraged Joni to give thanks in every situation as Paul had urged the Thessalonians. It wasn't easy but Joni persevered, even when she felt least like doing it. Her appearance mattered still more and Jay and Diana helped her to create a new image with make-up and suitable clothes which were attractive but comfortable for sitting in a wheel-chair.

Joni needed to be dressed and undressed each day. Being paralysed, she had no bladder control so someone had to empty the urine bag attached to her leg. It was easy to take her helpers for granted but Joni made strenuous efforts to express her thanks to close family and friends.

Other new pursuits gave Joni fresh pleasure. A musical group for voices and instruments met at Joni's house and eventually became sufficiently professional to sing at churches and rallies. She was asked to work as a counsellor at a Young Life club and then in the summer travelled to camp in Colorado. The girls were a little cautious of her at first but accepted her when they got to know her and saw how she identified with them.

Saying goodbye to Steve when he went off to college proved difficult. 'I'm going to miss you, Steve, but I'll keep praying for you. You've been such a help.'

Joni wouldn't have been normal if she hadn't secretly longed for a husband to share her life – not just anyone but someone who could come to terms with her handicap. Her singleness didn't rankle all the time, she tried hard to accept it as God's plan for her at least over that period. However, as one and then another friend married Joni felt lonely. 'Please God send me a friend to take away my loneliness.'

At this stage Don came into her life. She first met him at a Young Life leadership meeting but soon he became a constant visitor to her home and a regular escort to outside functions. 'Joni – I'm falling in love with you,' he confessed to her one day, words she had so often longed to hear yet, when uttered, made her feel afraid. Joni felt attracted to him and admired his spiritual maturity, but was this the man whom God had chosen as a husband for her? Could he cope with all her physical problems?

Others close to her were anxious too when she confided in them about the situation. 'Be careful, Joni,' warned Diana and Jay also expressed misgivings. They could see danger ahead and they were desperately anxious to avoid Joni getting hurt. Where would it all end? They longed for Joni to enjoy normal relationships but it would have to be a very special person to look after Joni for the rest of her life.

It was only natural for Joni to become thrilled at the prospect, so thrilled that complications began to arise. Joni found herself possessive, jealous of any other young girls with whom he came into contact. So much so that Don set off on a trip to Europe to give him a breathing-space. In spite of Joni's fears, he returned more loving than ever. It was he who encouraged Joni to pray for total healing, thinking perhaps it would make their future together easier.

Elders anointed her with oil. She attended healing services – all to no avail. Don and Joni prayed believingly but no miracle happened.

Finally Joni had to face the facts. It seemed extremely unlikely that God was going to heal her. Don grew quieter and more withdrawn and it was with Steve when he came home on vacation that Joni discussed her disappointment.

'Maybe God won't heal you until you receive

your glorified body,' he suggested thoughtfully one day.

'I can see that God does use our problems for His glory and our good,' replied Joni.

'Right, and your witness in your wheelchair may be even more effective than in your previously healthy state . . . think about it, Joni.'

And Joni did over the next few weeks, talking it over with Don too. So honest had she been with him that she was totally unprepared for the shock of his unexpected statement, 'I've got to leave you, Joni. We should never have thought about marriage. It wouldn't work in our circumstances.'

'You can't mean that, Don. Think it over . . . don't leave me.'

But the door closed and Don walked out of Joni's life.

'Why have you allowed this to happen, God?' was Joni's cry from the heart.

# 6: PTL – Praise the Lord

This time, however, Joni wasn't going to fall into another deep depression in this new crisis, but she felt hurt, angry and confused. Dick told her that Don had confided his doubts to him. Jay and Diana had certainly warned her against becoming too seriously involved but she had let her heart rule her head.

After the initial shock, she was eventually able to discuss it with Steve and she pored over the Bible to discover more about God and His dealings with people She found vital clues, but the old ones she had learned to value kept cropping up, 'In everything give thanks,' 'All things work together for good'. Could she apply these in her life there and then? God was putting her through one more test.

While accepting this, it still hurt when she learned that Don was falling in love with another woman. She felt neglected and alone. Would there ever be any more chances of happiness in her life? Yet, if God really loved her, He was not merely trying to thwart her but was interfering in the relationship because it didn't come in to His perfect blueprint for her future.

Slowly, she was able to appreciate what agony this step had caused Don too. It had been very difficult for him but through it all she had found that she had become free of all human props – precious as they all were to her – and must rely completely and utterly on God alone. Later, she was even able to congratulate Don and his fiancée Sandy with complete sincerity.

Friends who had feared the worst began to breathe again. Joni had weathered another storm. Like the Trapp family singers Joni held a deeply rooted conviction that if God closes a door, He opens a window. 'O.K. God. You've closed a door on a college career for me and also on marriage. What can you possibly have in mind for me then?' she prayed.

Joni was convinced God had a purpose in all her sufferings, it wasn't just a useless experience. At the time when this gap had appeared in her life she turned again to her art and began to take it seriously. Before it had just been a pleasant relaxation. The last thing in the world she wanted was for people to make a fuss of her drawings just because they had been done by a disabled person. She wanted them to be judged on their own merit.

Some were displayed in a local art festival which gave Joni a great deal of pleasure. She started experimenting with different art forms and materials. The original idea was to give her drawings as presents to friends and she enjoyed the creativity but never made any profit out of them.

One day, however, Neill Miller, a Christian businessman, saw some drawings in Mr. Eareckson's office. He was so impressed he made arrangements to hold a small exhibition in a local restaurant. It was a runaway success. Much to her surprise, television reporters were waiting to interview her and she was presented with a bouquet. Joni felt embarrassed at first until she realised peoples' interest and praise was genuine.

Folks flocked around to ask questions and then stayed to buy examples of her art. By the evening she was staggered to learn she had sold about a thousand dollars' worth of drawings. As a result,

Joni was asked to appear on a local television programme.

'Why do you put the letters PTL on every drawing?' asked the reporter.

'It means – Praise the Lord. God cares for everyone and I am personally thankful for His goodness to me. Without His help, I would never have managed as a paraplegic.'

This opened the door to many other functions. Joni made sure she shared her Christian views while she displayed her art work, whether at clubs, schools or church groups. She even left a drawing at the White House for the President's wife, Mrs. Nixon. The old inarticulate, tongue-tied Joni had disappeared for ever.

A worthwhile spin-off from all these appearances was the money Joni started to earn which gave her a chance not only to become independent financially but start a greeting-card company called Joni PTL and also set up a Christian bookstore with two other partners. Finance, though, was never the most important factor. Joni always made sure that people were made aware of her Christian testimony, often personally handing out a leaflet she had written. The goods in the shop were displayed attractively to attract shoppers to browse among worthwhile Christian literature.

It all seemed a long way from the days when Joni lay helpless on a Stryker frame, bald, unable to move and devoid of hope for the future. But even she couldn't have forecast the next development. The telephone rang one morning. 'Can you come and tell your story and show your drawings on the 'Today Show' in New York?

Wow! An exciting and formidable challenge but Joni hardly hesitated before accepting the invitation. Friends accompanied her on the journey and Miss Walters, the interviewer, put Joni at her ease immediately. She was given every opportunity to say everything she had in mind. Joni warmed to her and so felt relaxed and at ease in spite of the lights and the cameras.

Other exhibitions followed, sponsored by the pen company whose products she used in her art work. Newspapers clamoured for articles. Secular and Christian periodicals mailed requests for more interviews. Local radio and television shows expressed their interest. Suddenly Joni was becoming a well-known national figure. Being made aware of this, she was determined to exploit the situation to the full, not for her own interests but to glorify the Lord.

As her opportunities to speak became more frequent and her audiences larger, Joni relished the chance to discuss her accident with teenagers.

'No, I don't think God did it to punish me – that's not the way that He works. But I do know that I wouldn't change places with anyone else in the world. Oh, I didn't think that way at first, of course. For a long time I felt bitter, disillusioned about life and extremely depressed. But through it all, I've drawn much closer to Him and He's given me some very exciting work to do. I just praise Him that He changed the rebellious teenager I used to be. Where was my behaviour leading me? I shudder to think if He had not intervened at that stage.'

Joni has surprised herself and her friends and family with the range of her achievements over the last few years. In 1976, her autobiography, Joni, was published and it received wide international acclaim, probably because of its arresting honesty and its clear description of Joni's spiritual journey.

So many people wrote in who had suffered similar experiences that Joni felt compelled to write a second book, A Step Further, in conjunction with her friend, Steve Estes. It didn't contain any more details about Joni's life, but further reflections and comments on the question of suffering.

In time, the book was featured in a film by World Wide Pictures. Still more films, including

Perfections of His Love and a four-part series called Blessings out of Brokenness, are being released throughout the United States of America. They all deal with the problems of suffering and disablement but try to foster relationships between the able-bodied and the disabled.

A new organisation, Joni and Friends, was set up in 1979, as an outreach to churches helping people with physical disabilities. Joni and Friends is keen to make churches aware of the needs of handicapped people. They organise seminars on the subject and distribute literature. Also they encourage ministers to use the talents of the disabled members of their congregations, believing that they have an important contribution to make in the community. Because they have lost their mobility, it does not mean to say that they have been stripped of their talents. On the contrary, often the reverse is true and they have more time to cultivate their gifts when they are confined to a wheelchair.

Joni is also responsible for a five-minute radio programme beamed over 175 radio stations which seeks to enlighten the general public about different disabilities.

Another training programme goes under the name of People Plus. This is specifically designed to teach able-bodied people how to assist the disabled. These skills are taught twice a year at California State University.

Joni has built up a counselling service to cover a wide range of questions from the spiritual to the purely practical, embracing subjects like aids and government help. For too long they believed the needs and problems of the disabled had been swept under the carpet and the people themselves kept discreetly in the background.

As well as for her drawings, Joni is now renowned for her two record albums, Joni's Song and Spirit Wings.

Another highlight in Joni's life occurred on July 3rd, 1982, when she married Ken Tada of Burbank, California, who is a high school history and physical education teacher. He is a director on the board of Joni and Friends and they live at Woodland Hills, California.

Joni has travelled extensively, both at home and abroad. Recently she made a tour of Britain followed afterwards by a trip to Poland where her visit made a great impact. She believes it is right to accept invitations like these, in spite of the limitations of being a paraplegic, because it gives her the chance to take the message of God's love and concern for dispirited, disillusioned and desperately lonely disabled people.

Like the apostle Paul two thousand years ago, she firmly believes that 'I can do all things through Christ who strengthens me.'

And the only possible ending to the story of Joni's rich and eventful life is the phrase that is printed on each of her inspiring drawings – P.T.L. – Praise the Lord.

If you wish to receive *regular
information* about *new books*,
please send your name and address
to:—
London Bible Warehouse
PO Box 123
Basingstoke
Hants RG23 7NL

Name: . . . . . . . . . . . . . . . . . . . . . . . . . . . . . . . . . . . . . . .
Address: . . . . . . . . . . . . . . . . . . . . . . . . . . . . . . . . . . . . .
. . . . . . . . . . . . . . . . . . . . . . . . . . . . . . . . . . . . . . . . . . . . .
. . . . . . . . . . . . . . . . . . . . . . . . . . . . . . . . . . . . . . . . . . . . .
. . . . . . . . . . . . . . . . . . . . . . . . . . . . . . . . . . . . . . . . . . . . .

I am especially interested in:—

Music/Theology/"Popular"
Paperbacks
Delete which do not apply

P.S. If you have ideas for new Christian Books or
other products, Please write to us too!